EASY PIANO

BARRY MANILOW
GREATEST HITS

Cover photo/Getty Images Entertainment
Photographer: Tim Mosenfelder

ISBN 978-1-4950-9838-3

HAL•LEONARD®

7777 W. BLUEMOUND RD. P.O. BOX 13819 MILWAUKEE, WI 53213

Visit Hal Leonard Online at
www.halleonard.com

BANDSTAND BOOGIE
from the Television Series AMERICAN BANDSTAND

Special Lyric by BARRY MANILOW and BRUCE SUSSMAN
Music by CHARLES ALBERTINE

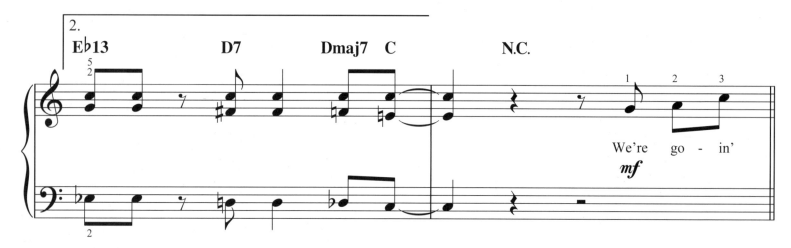

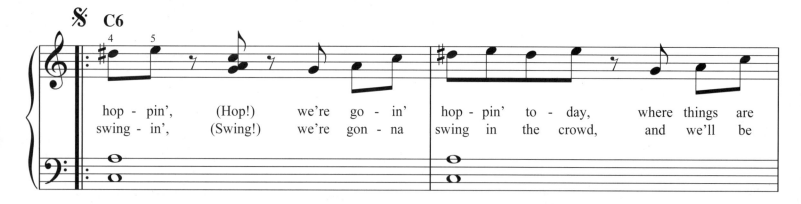

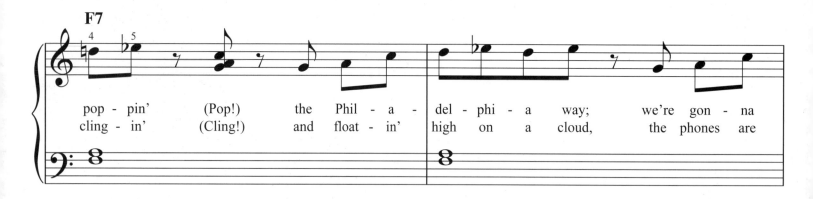

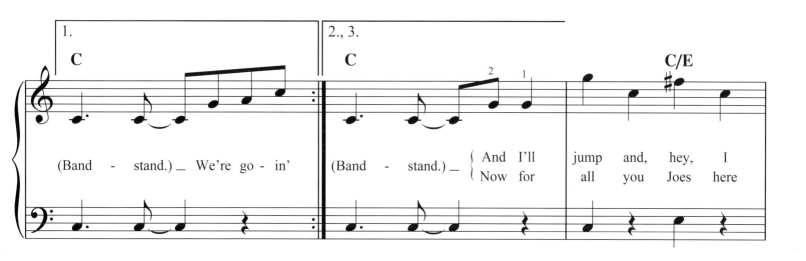

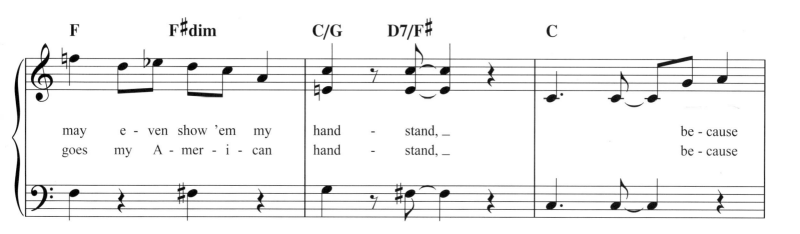

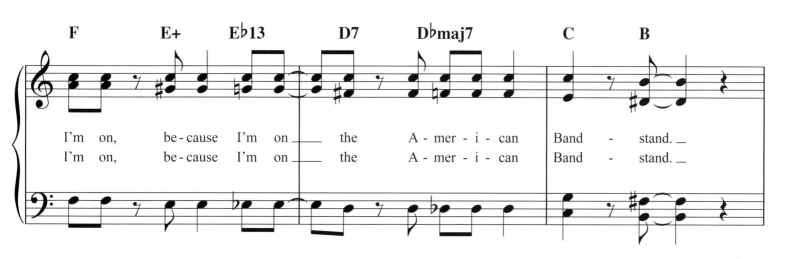

When we   dance   real   slow   I'll   show   all   the   guys   in   the
As   we   dance   real   slow   I'm   show - in'   the   guys   in   the

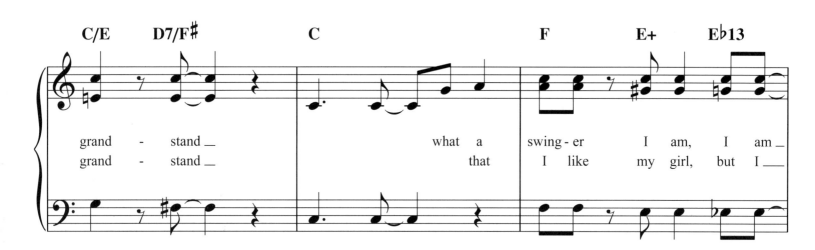

grand - stand __   what   a   swing - er   I   am,   I   am __
grand - stand __   that   I   like   my   girl,   but   I __

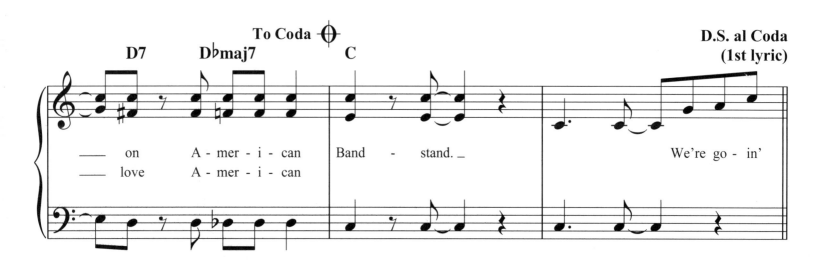

To Coda

D.S. al Coda
(1st lyric)

__ on   A - mer - i - can   Band - stand. __   We're go - in'
__ love   A - mer - i - can

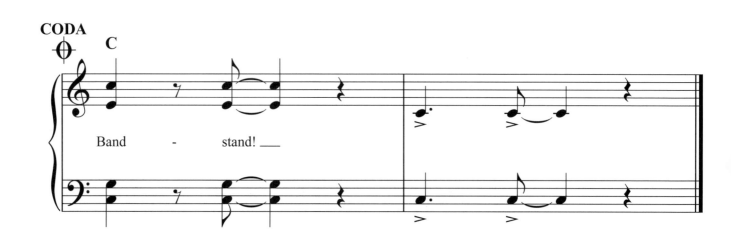

CODA

Band - stand! __

COPACABANA
(At the Copa)
from Barry Manilow's COPACABANA

Music by BARRY MANILOW
Lyric by BRUCE SUSSMAN and JACK FELDMAN

Moderately, with a Latin feel

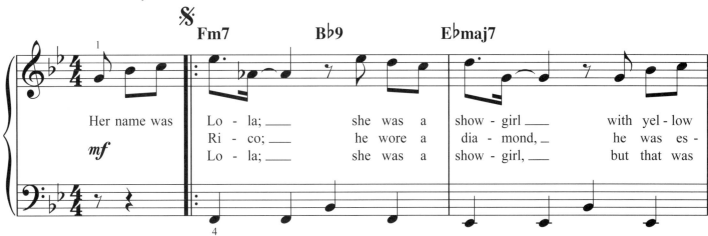

Her name was Lo - la; ___ she was a show - girl ___ with yel - low
Ri - co; ___ he wore a dia - mond, ___ he was es -
Lo - la; ___ she was a show - girl, ___ but that was

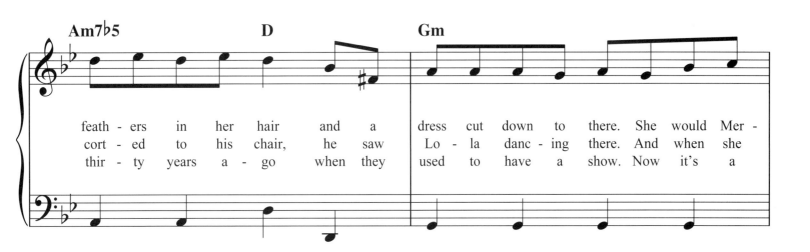

feath - ers in her hair and a dress cut down to there. She would Mer -
cort - ed to his chair, he saw Lo - la danc - ing there. And when she
thir - ty years a - go when they used to have a show. Now it's a

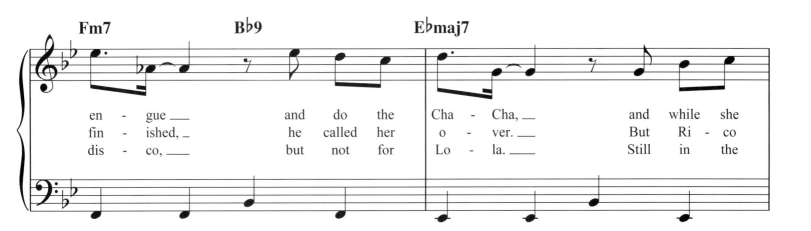

en - gue ___ and do the Cha - Cha, ___ and while she
fin - ished, ___ he called her o - ver. ___ But Ri - co
dis - co, ___ but not for Lo - la. ___ Still in the

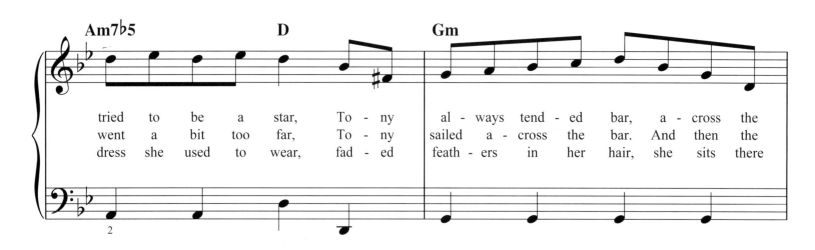

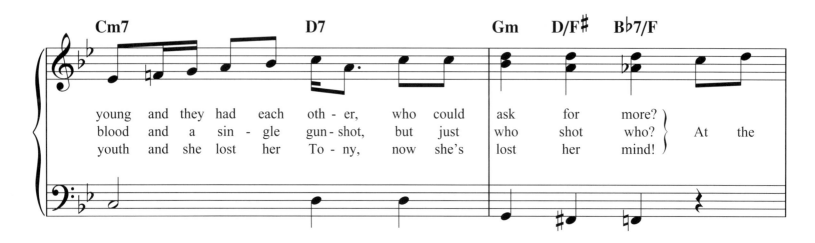

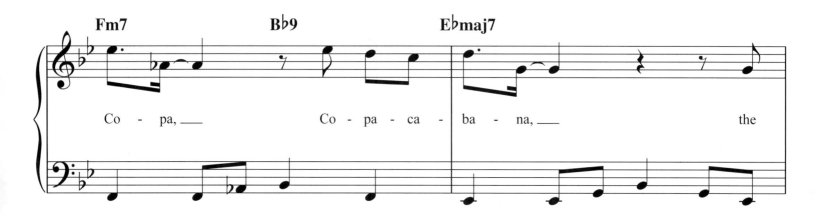

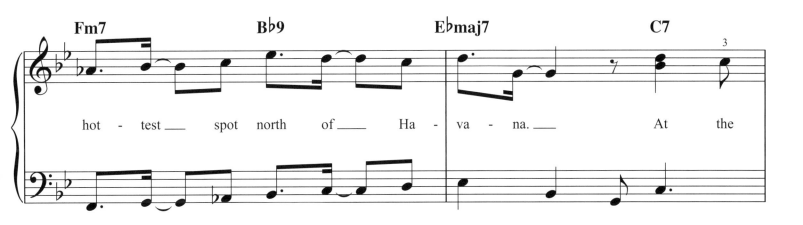

hot - test spot north of Ha - va - na. At the

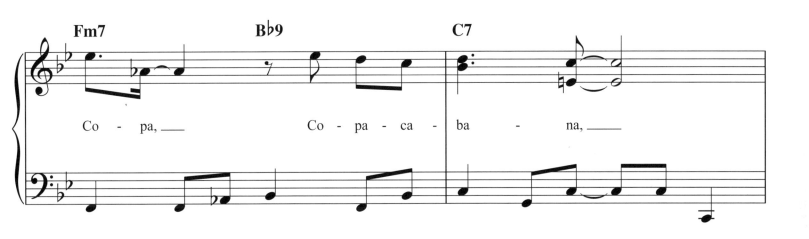

Co - pa, Co - pa - ca - ba - na,

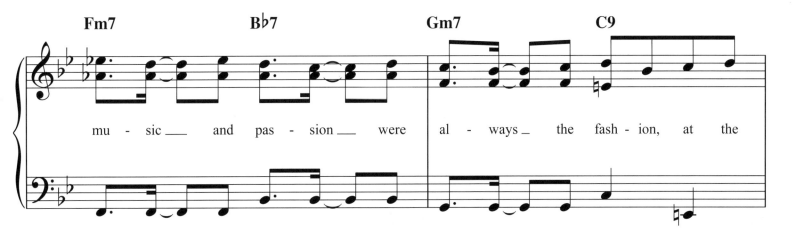

mu - sic and pas - sion were al - ways the fash - ion, at the

To Coda ⊕

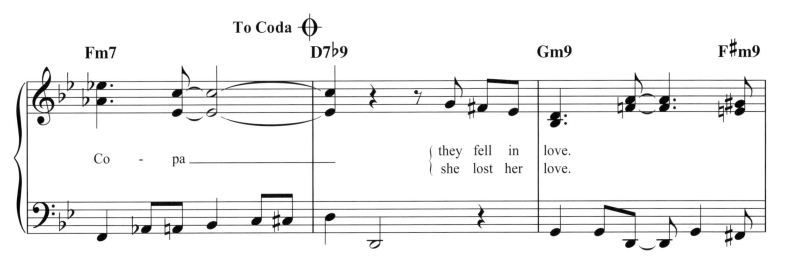

Co - pa they fell in love. / she lost her love.

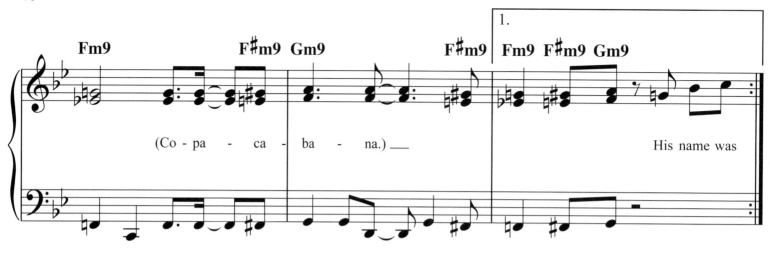

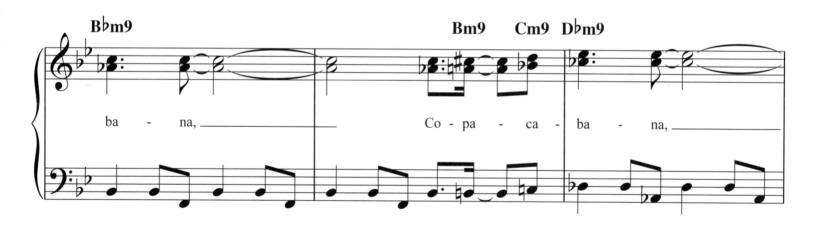

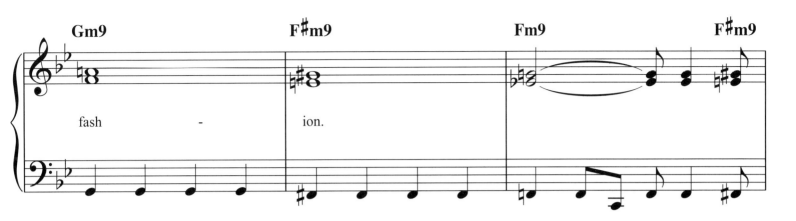

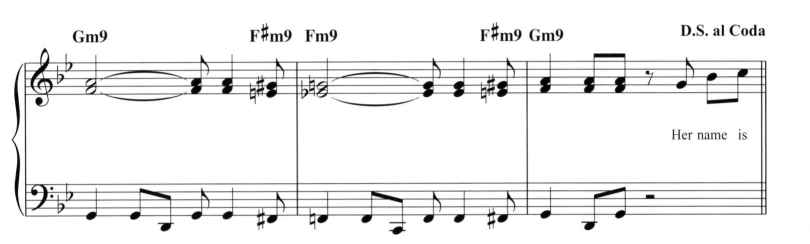

CAN'T SMILE WITHOUT YOU

Words and Music by CHRIS ARNOLD,
DAVID MARTIN and GEOFF MORROW

13

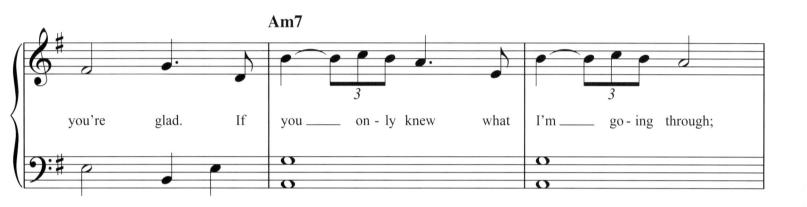

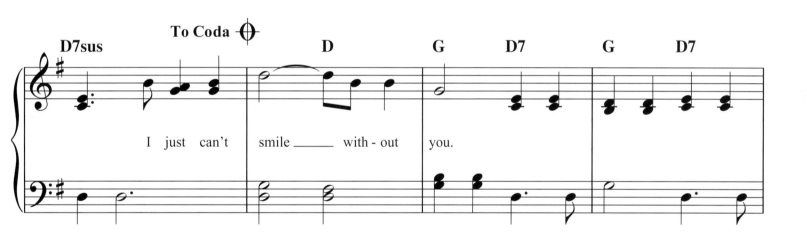

Who'd-a be-lieved that you were part of a dream? _ Now it all seems _

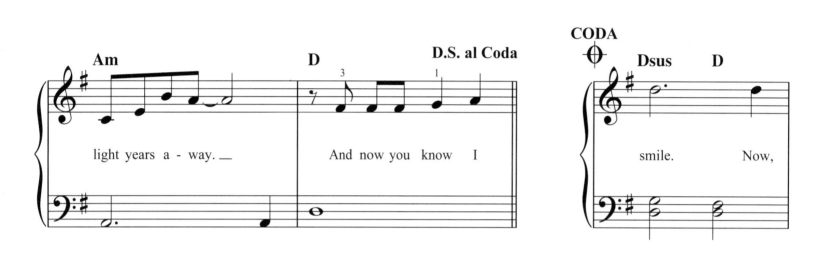

light years a - way. _ And now you know I smile. Now,

some peo-ple say _ hap-pi-ness takes _ so ver-y long to

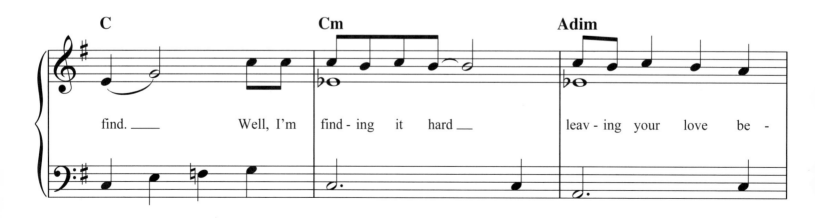

find. _ Well, I'm find-ing it hard _ leav-ing your love be -

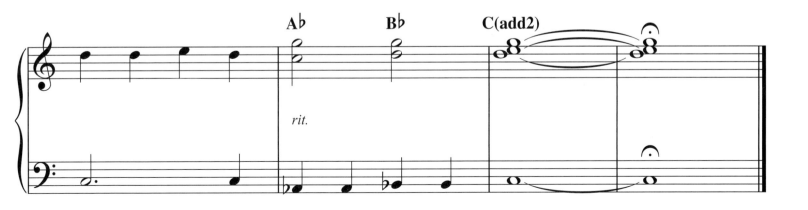

LOOKS LIKE WE MADE IT

Words and Music by RICHARD KERR
and WILL JENNINGS

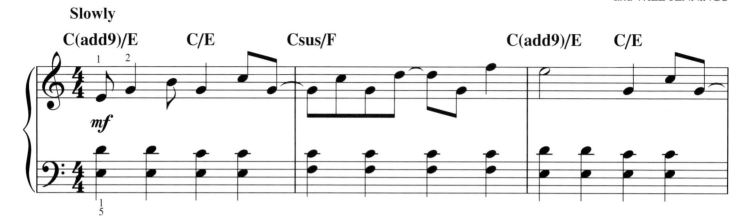

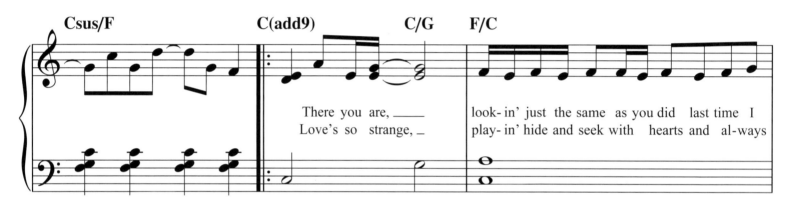

There you are, _____ look-in' just the same as you did last time I
Love's so strange, _ play-in' hide and seek with hearts and al-ways

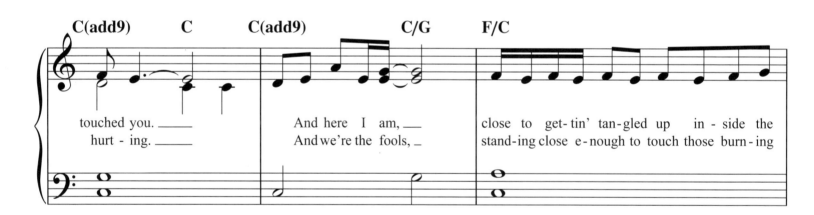

touched you. _____ And here I am, _____ close to get-tin' tan-gled up in - side the
hurt - ing. _____ And we're the fools, _ stand-ing close e-nough to touch those burn-ing

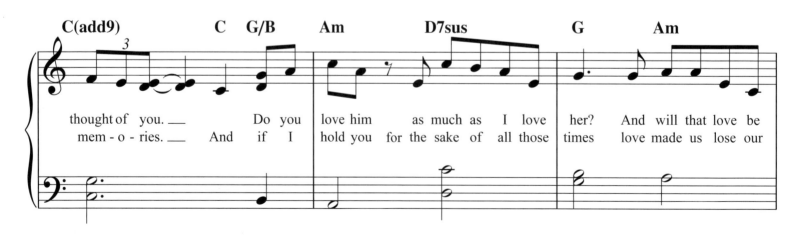

thought of you. _ Do you love him as much as I love her? And will that love be
mem - o - ries. _ And if I hold you for the sake of all those times love made us lose our

strong when old feel-ings start to / minds, could I ev-er let you | stir? ___ Looks like we / go? ___ Oh, no we've | made it, / made it, | left each

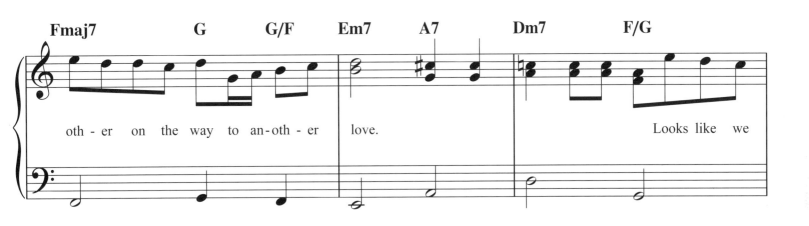

oth-er on the way to an-oth-er | love. | Looks like we

made it, or I | thought so till to-day un-til you were | there, ___ ev-'ry-where, and

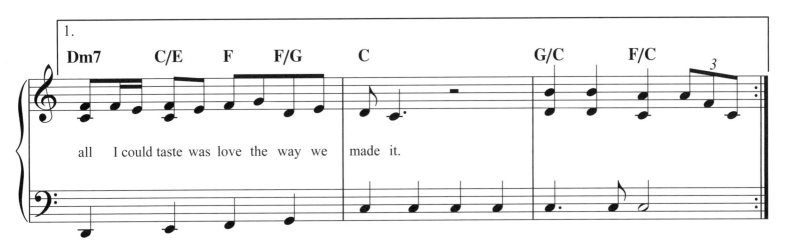

1.

all I could taste was love the way we | made it.

18

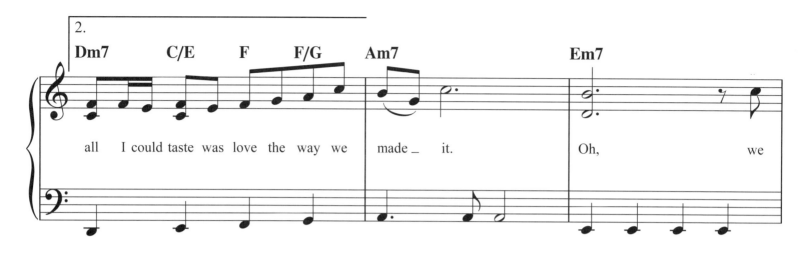

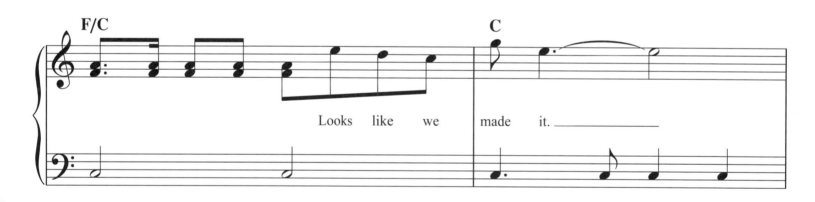

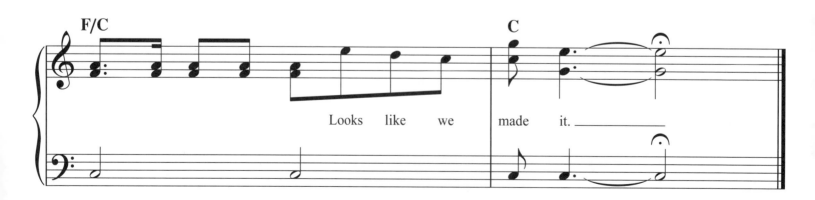

COULD IT BE MAGIC

Inspired by "Prelude in C Minor" by F. CHOPIN
Words and Music by BARRY MANILOW
and ADRIENNE ANDERSON

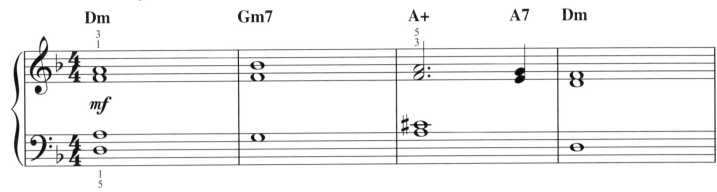

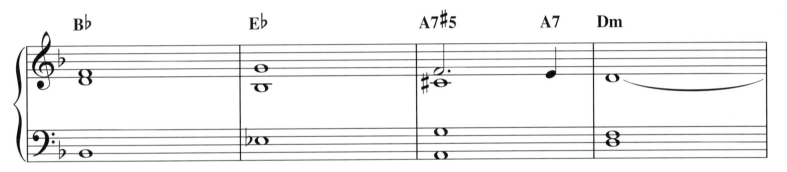

Spir - it, move _____ me
La - dy, take _____ me

ev - 'ry time _____ I'm
high up - on _____ a

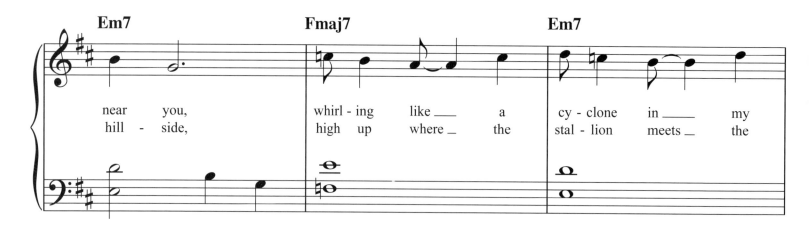

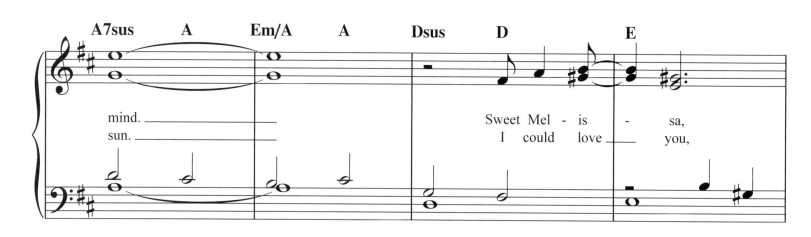

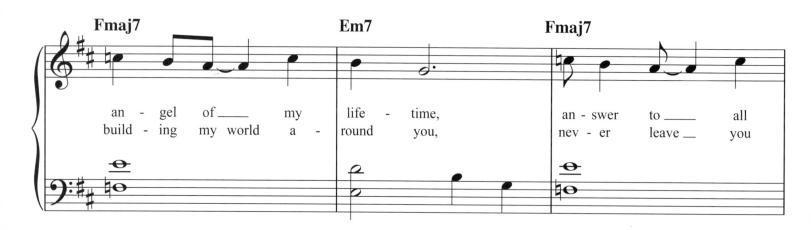

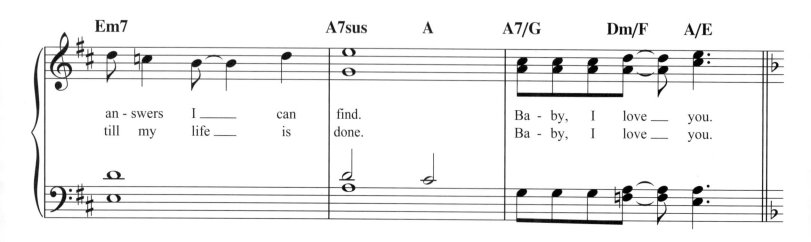

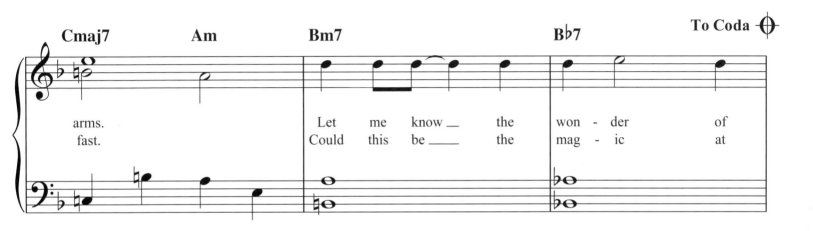

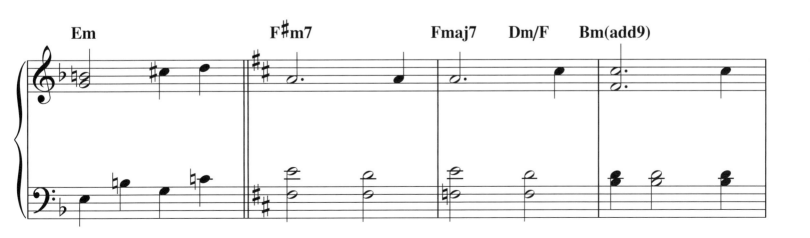

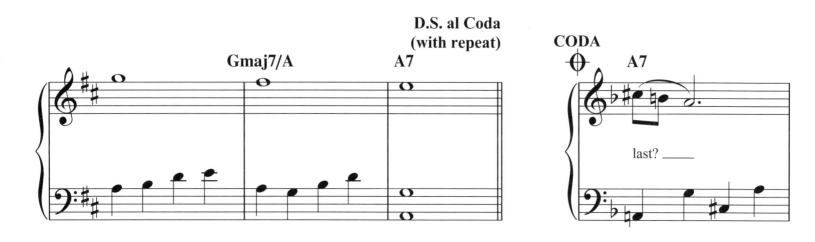

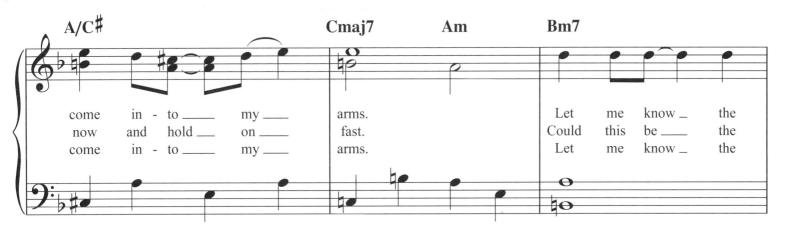

come in - to _____ my _____ arms.
now and hold _____ on _____ fast.
come in - to _____ my _____ arms.

Let me know __ the
Could this be _____ the
Let me know __ the

won - der of all ____ of you. __
mag - ic at last? ____
won - der of all ____ of you. __

Ba - by, I want __ you
Could it be mag - ic?

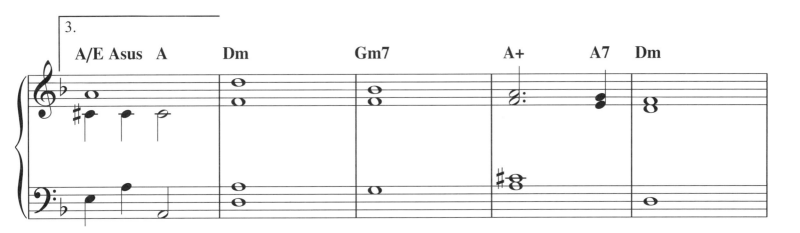

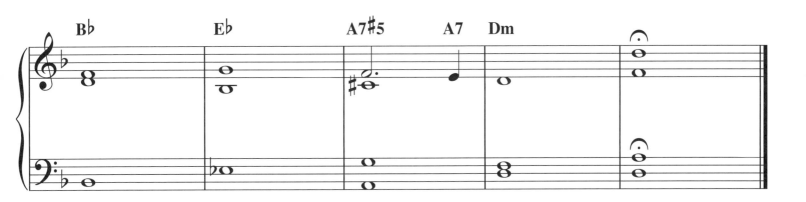

EVEN NOW

Lyric by MARTY PANZER
Music by BARRY MANILOW

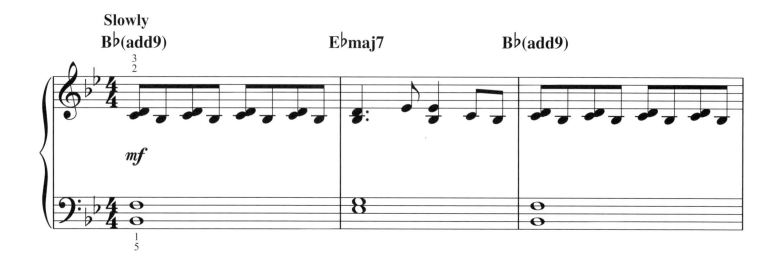

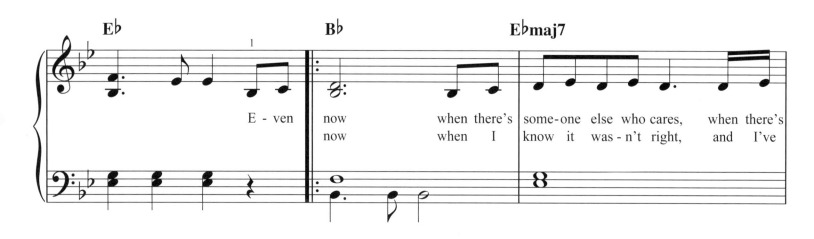

E - ven now when there's some-one else who cares, when there's
now when I know it was-n't right, and I've

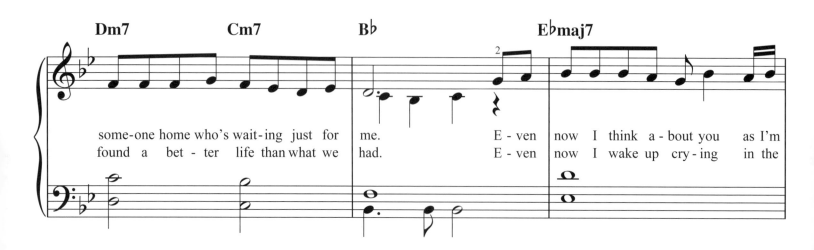

some-one home who's wait-ing just for me. E - ven now I think a-bout you as I'm
found a bet-ter life than what we had. E - ven now I wake up cry-ing in the

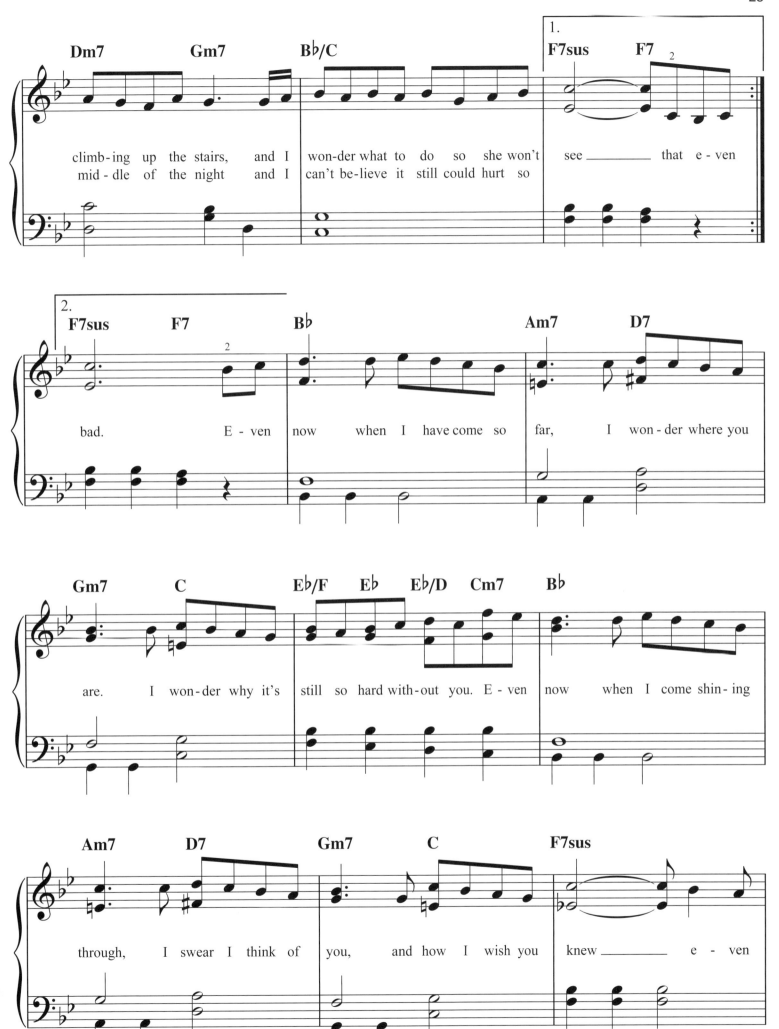

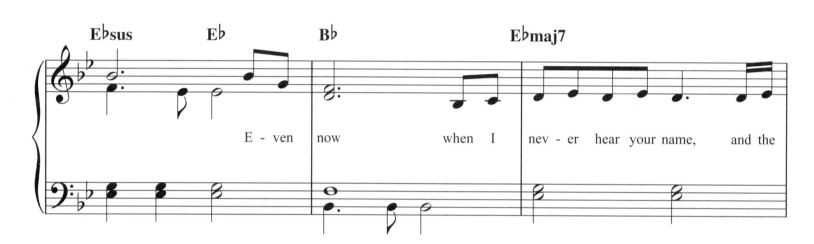

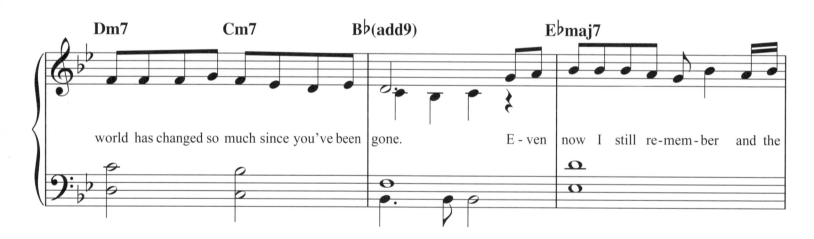

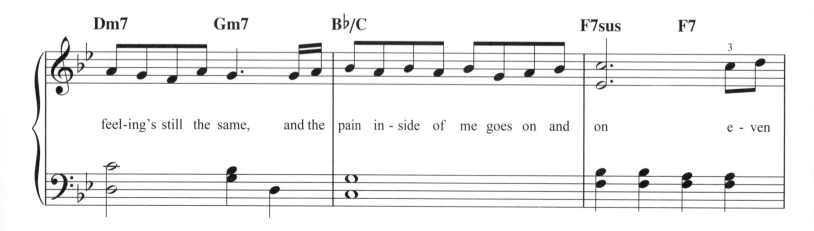

now. E - ven now when I have come so far, I won-der where you

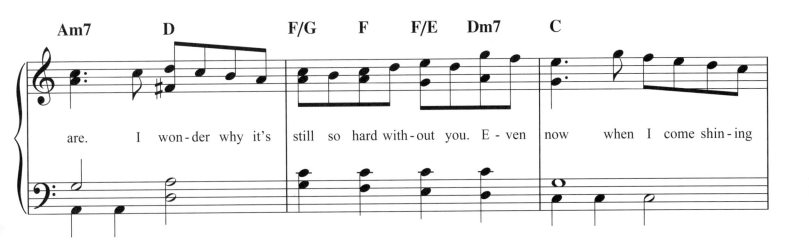

are. I won-der why it's still so hard with-out you. E - ven now when I come shin-ing

through, I swear I think of you, and God, I wish you knew _____ some-

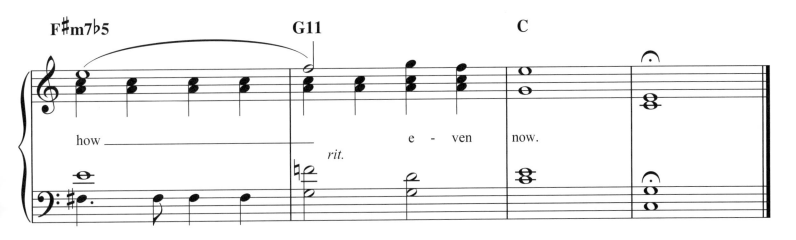

how _____ e - ven now.

I MADE IT THROUGH THE RAIN

Words and Music by BARRY MANILOW,
JACK FELDMAN, BRUCE SUSSMAN,
DREY SHEPPERD and GERARD KENNY

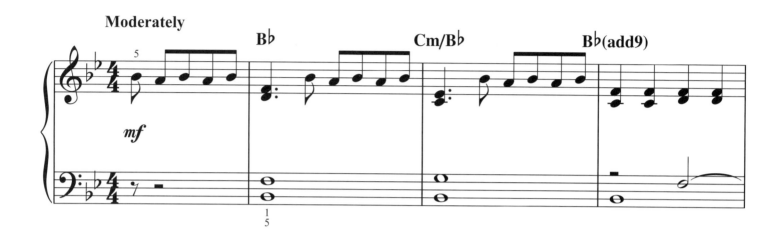

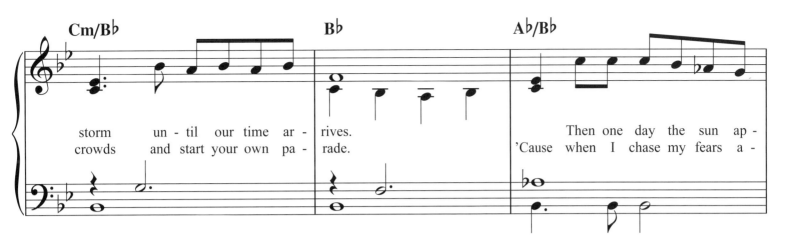

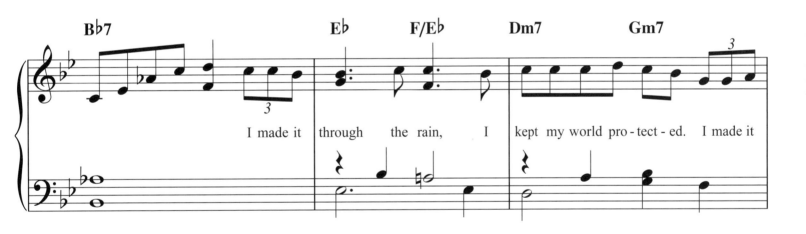

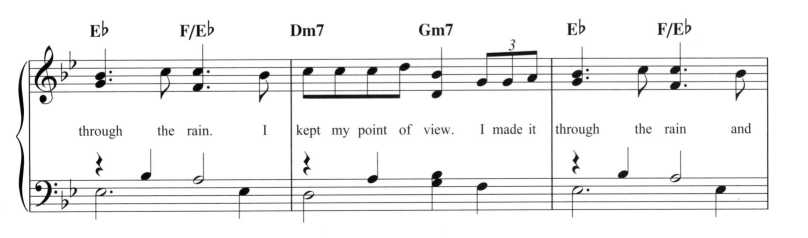

found my-self re-spect-ed   by the   oth-ers who _____ got   rained on   too ___   and

made it   through. _____

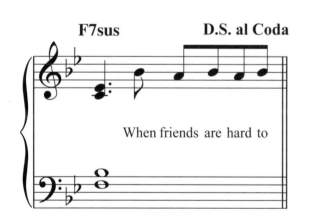

When friends are hard to

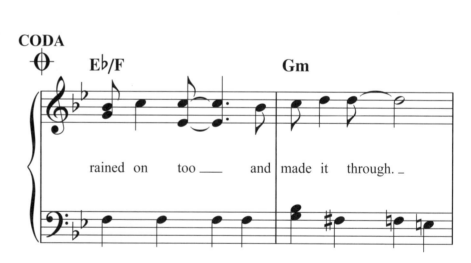

rained on   too ___ and made it   through. _

I made it   through   the rain,   I kept my world pro-tect-ed. I made it

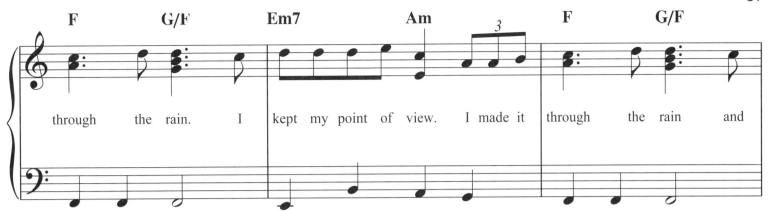

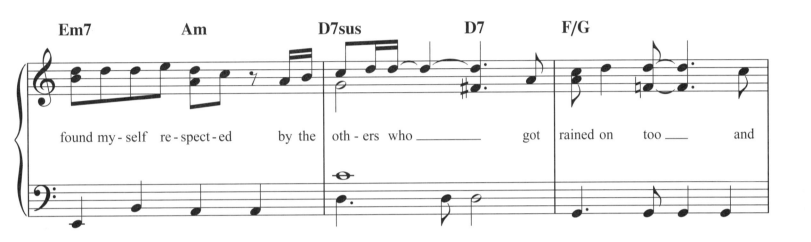

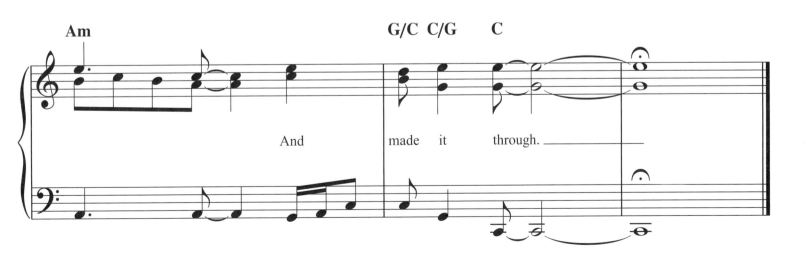

I WRITE THE SONGS

Words and Music by
BRUCE JOHNSTON

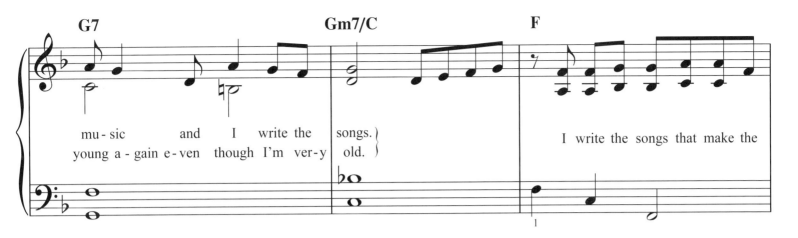

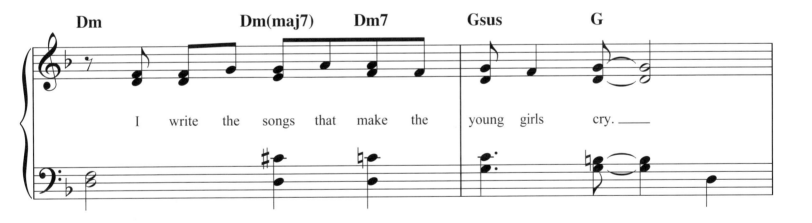

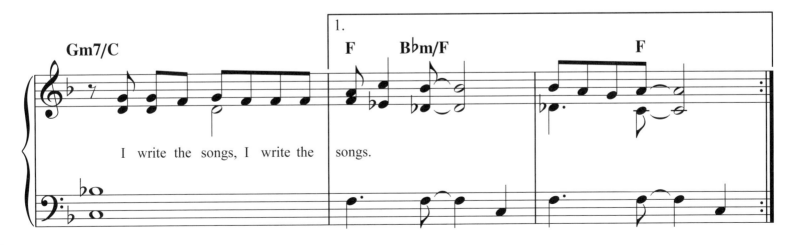

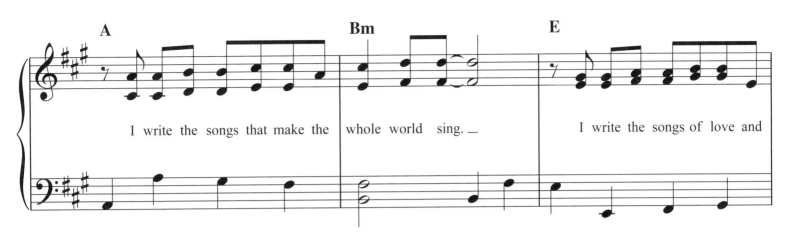

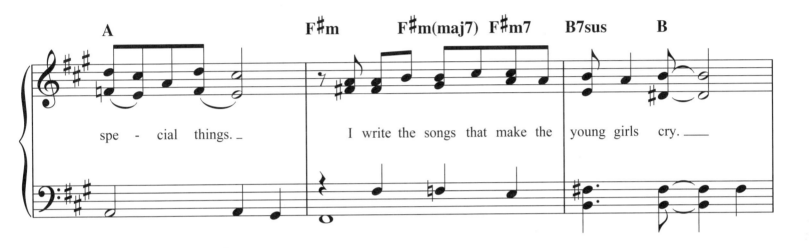

MANDY

Words and Music by SCOTT ENGLISH
and RICHARD KERR

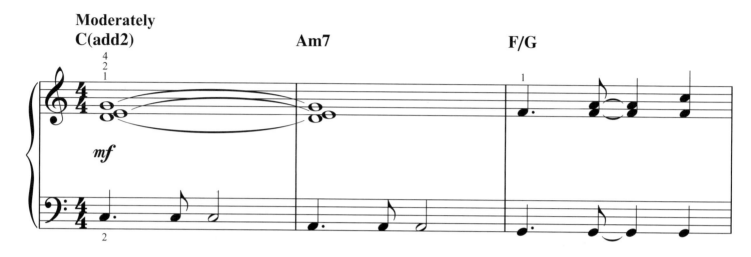

I re-mem-ber all my life, _____
morn-ing. Just an-oth-er day, _____
stand-ing on the edge of time, _____ I've

rain-ing down as cold as ice, _____
hap-py peo-ple pass my way. _____
walked a-way when love was mine.

shad-ows of a man, a
Look-ing in their eyes, I
Caught up in a world of

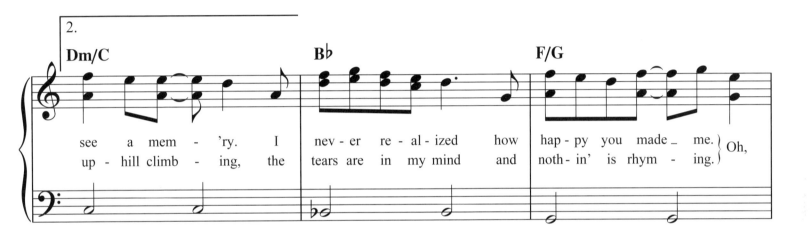

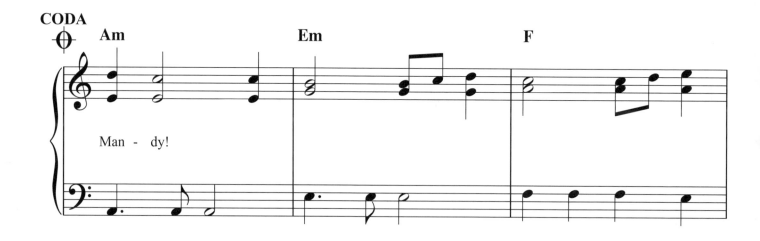

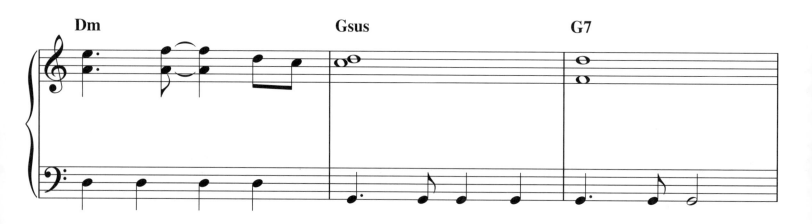

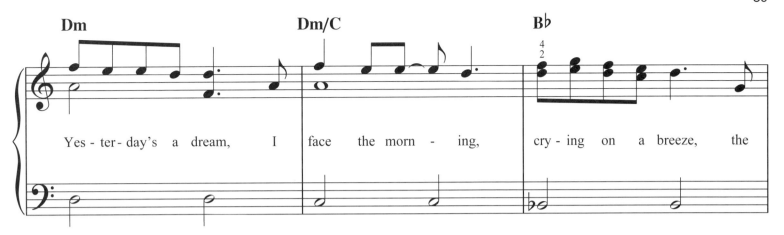

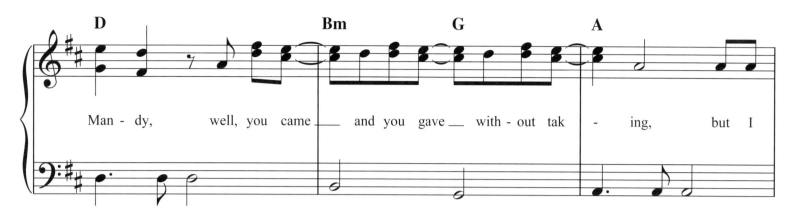

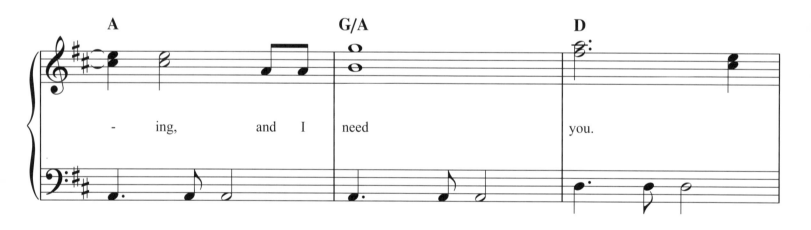

SOMEWHERE IN THE NIGHT

Words and Music by WILL JENNINGS
and RICHARD KERR

To Coda ⊕

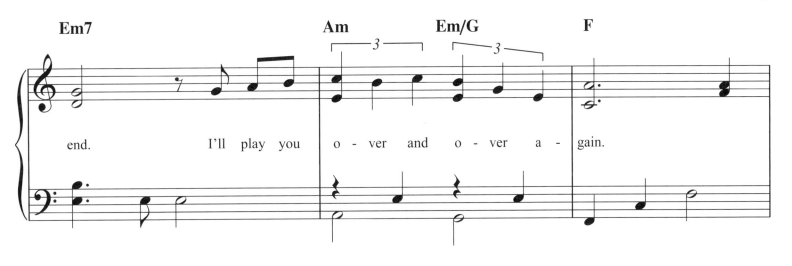

end.   I'll play you   o - ver and o - ver a - gain.

Lov - ing so warm, __   mov - ing so right, __   clos - ing your eyes __   and

feel - ing the light.   We'll just go on burn - ing   bright, __   some-where in the

night.   You'll

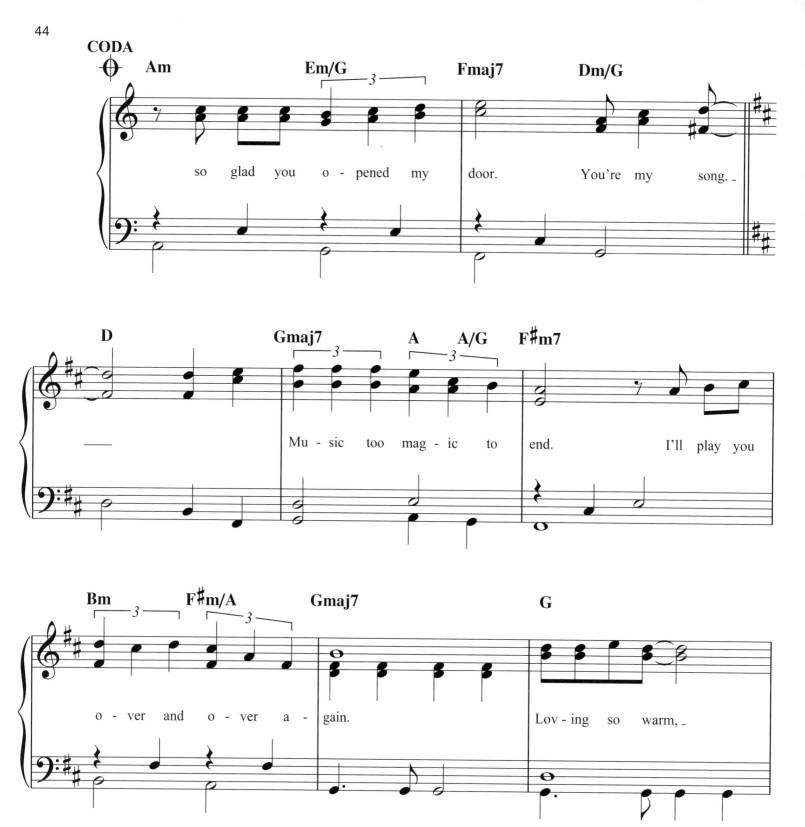

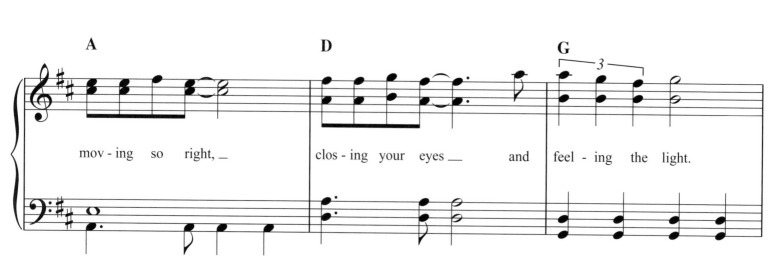

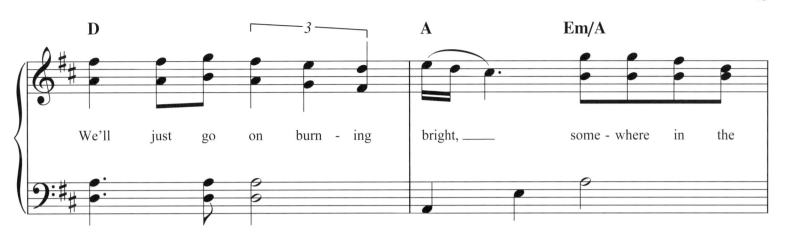

We'll just go on burn - ing bright, _____ some - where in the

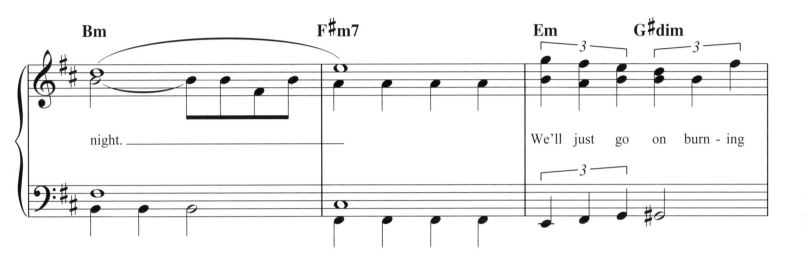

night. _____ We'll just go on burn - ing

bright some - where in the night.

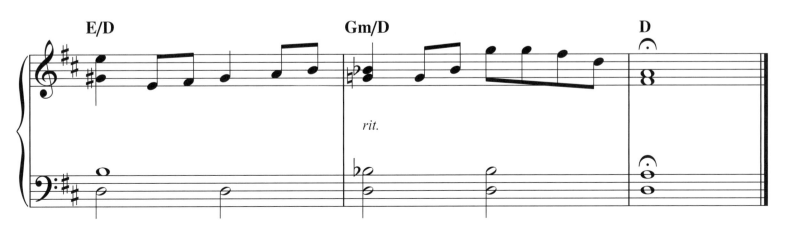

READY TO TAKE A CHANCE AGAIN

from the Paramount Picture FOUL PLAY

Words by NORMAN GIMBEL
Music by CHARLES FOX

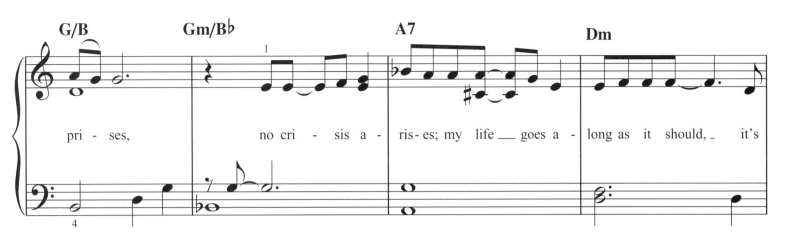

pri - ses, no cri - sis a - ris - es; my life ___ goes a - long as it should, ___ it's

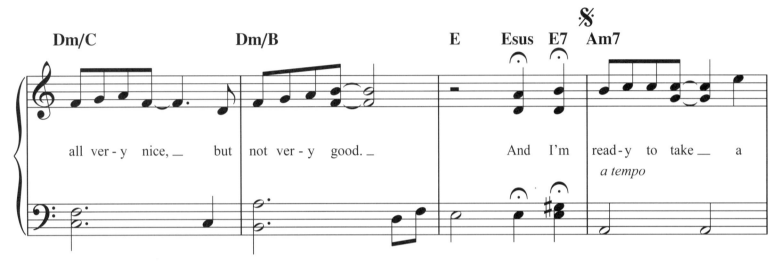

all ver - y nice, ___ but not ver - y good. ___ And I'm read - y to take ___ a

a tempo

chance a - gain, ___ read - y to put ___ my love on the line ___ with you. Been

To Coda ⊕

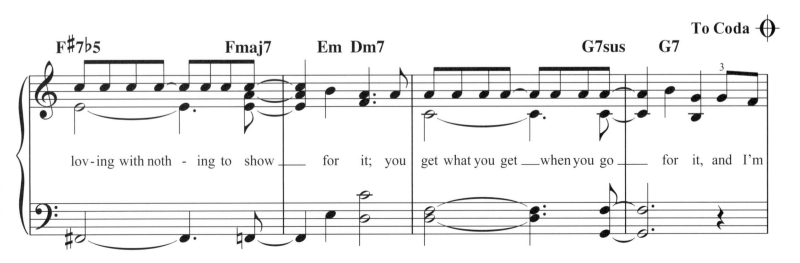

lov - ing with noth - ing to show ___ for it; you get what you get ___ when you go ___ for it, and I'm

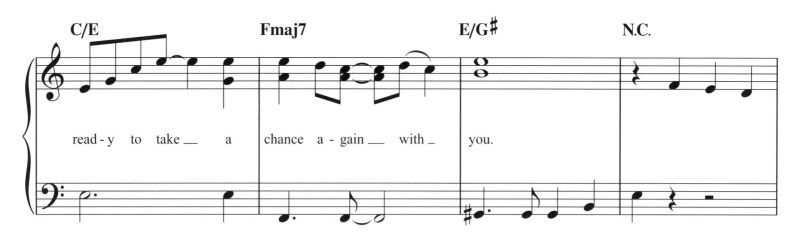

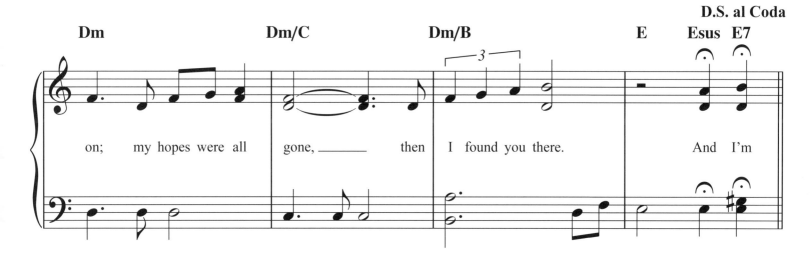

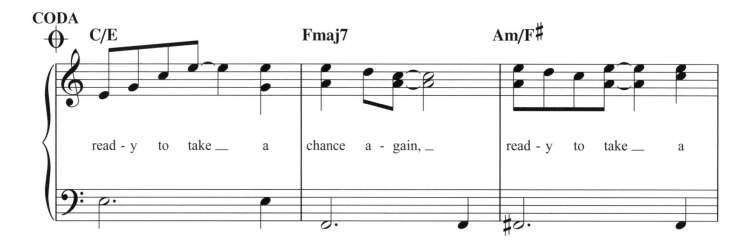

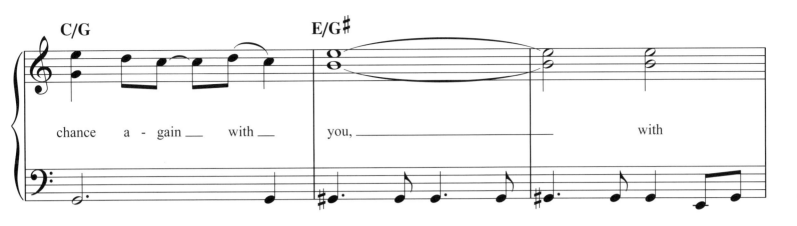

chance a - gain ___ with ___ you, _____ with

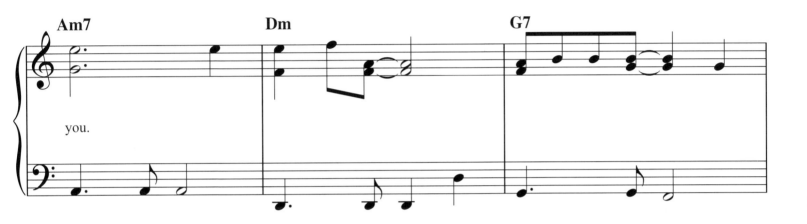

you.

Repeat and Fade | **Optional Ending**

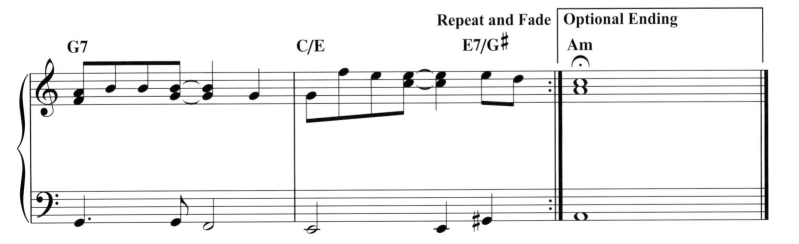

SOMEWHERE DOWN THE ROAD

Words and Music by CYNTHIA WEIL
and TOM SNOW

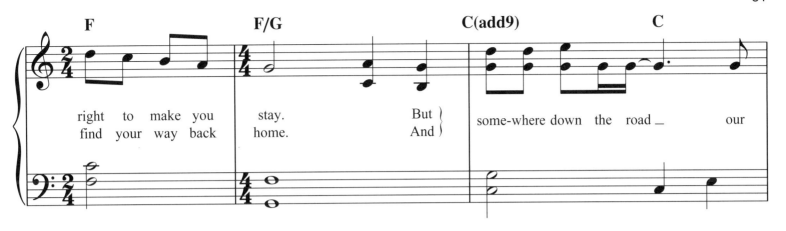

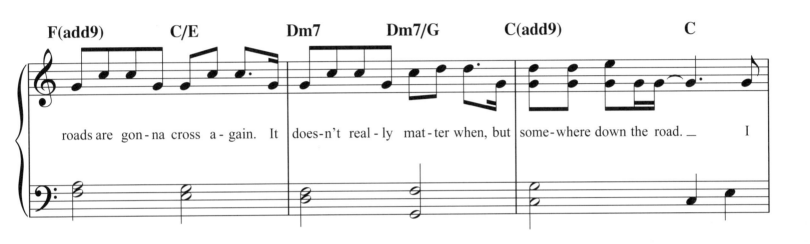

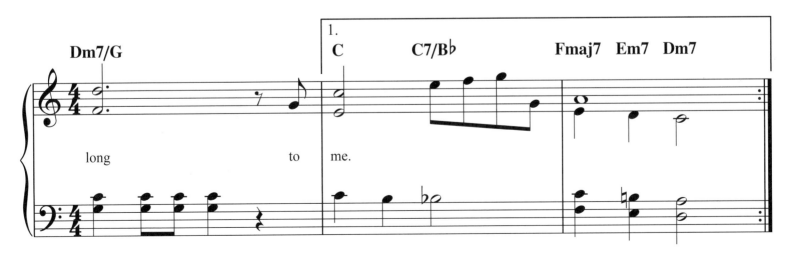

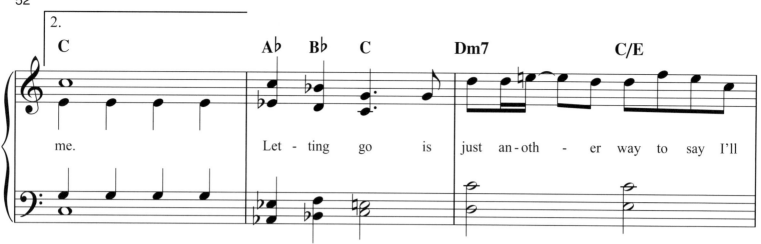

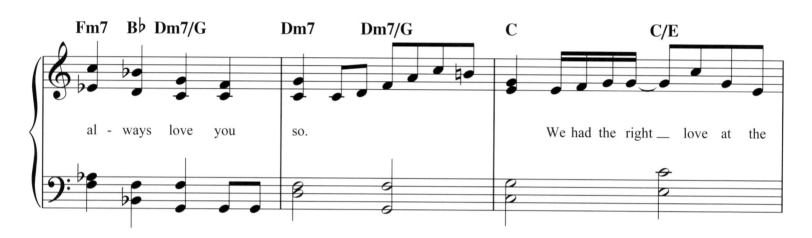

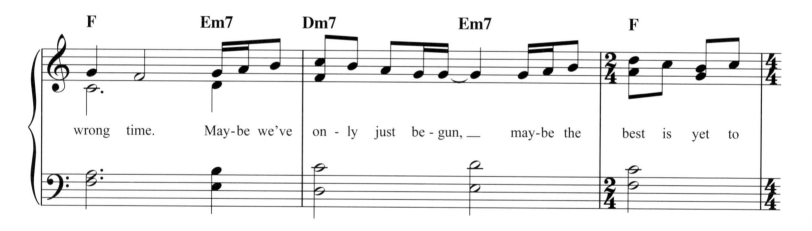

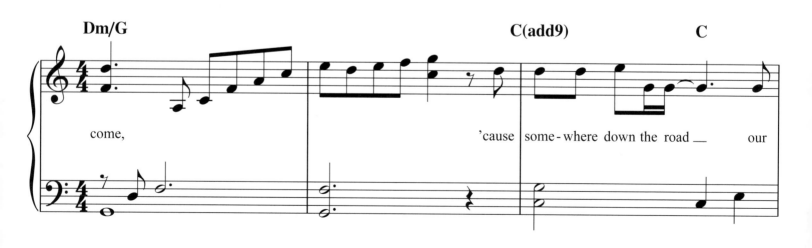

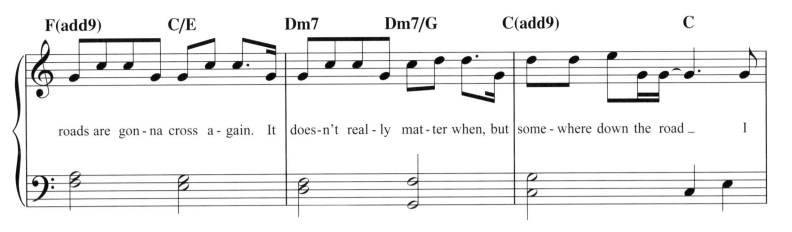

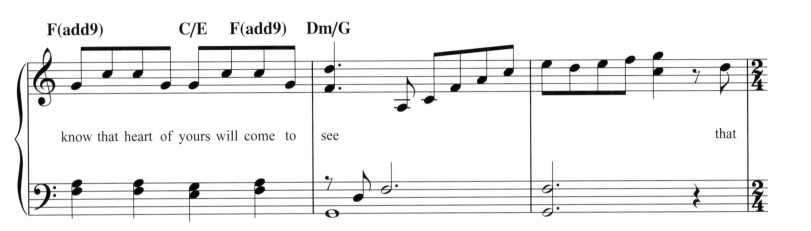

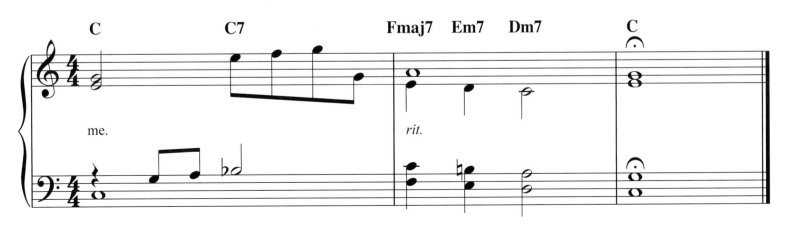

THIS ONE'S FOR YOU

Lyric by MARTY PANZER
Music by BARRY MANILOW

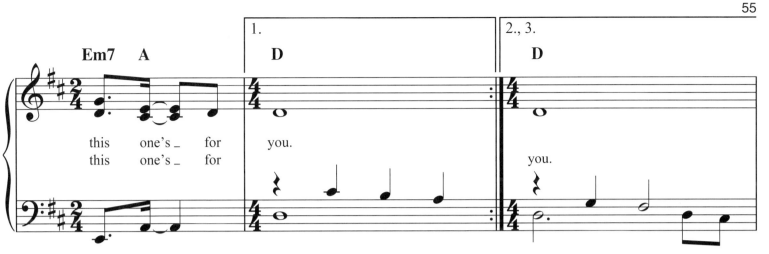

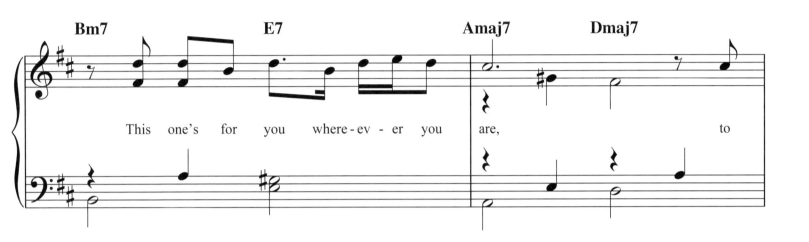

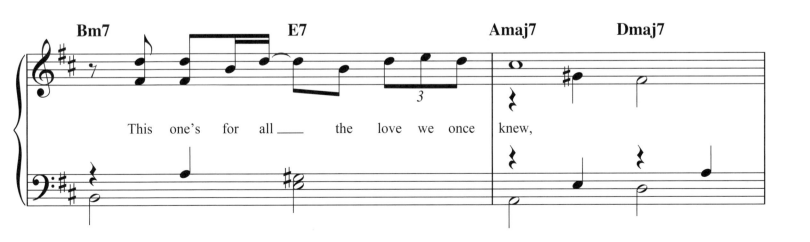

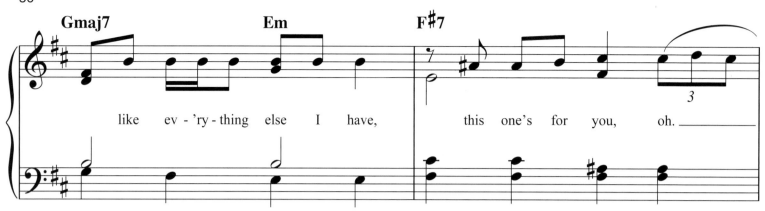

like ev - 'ry - thing else I have, this one's for you, oh. _____

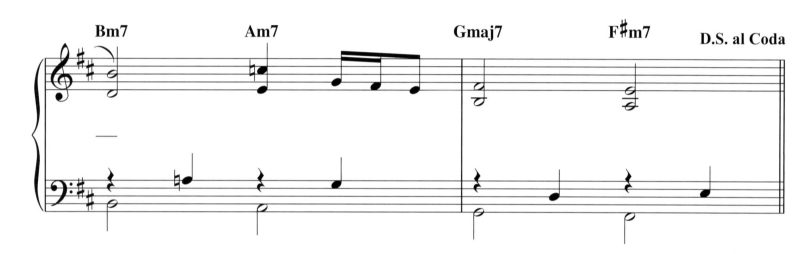

D.S. al Coda

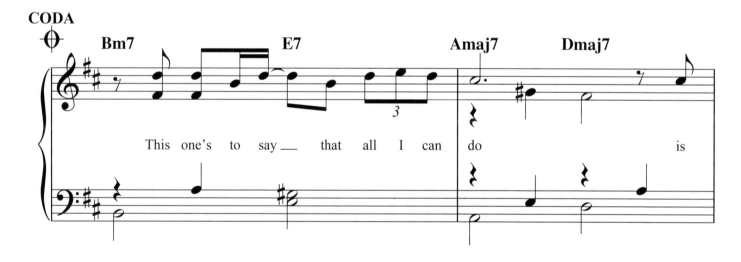

CODA

This one's to say ___ that all I can do is

hope that you ___ will hear me sing ___ 'cause this one's for you. ___ Oh, _____

This one's for you ___ where - ev - er you are, to

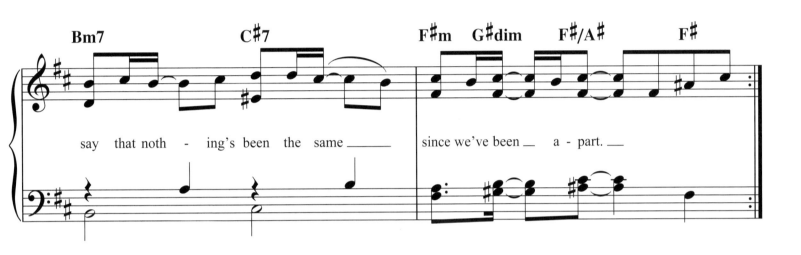

say that noth - ing's been the same ___ since we've been ___ a - part. ___

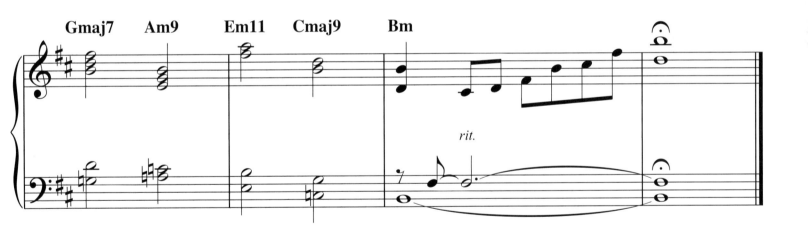

rit.

Additional Lyrics

3. I've got it all it seems, for all it means to me,
But I sing of things I miss and things that used to be.
And I wonder ev'ry night if you might just miss me too.
And I sing for you, I sing for you.

WEEKEND IN NEW ENGLAND

Words and Music by
RANDY EDELMAN

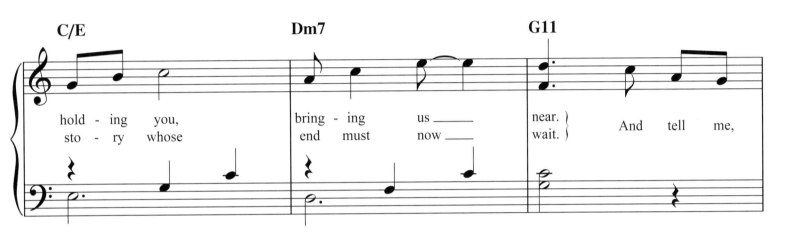

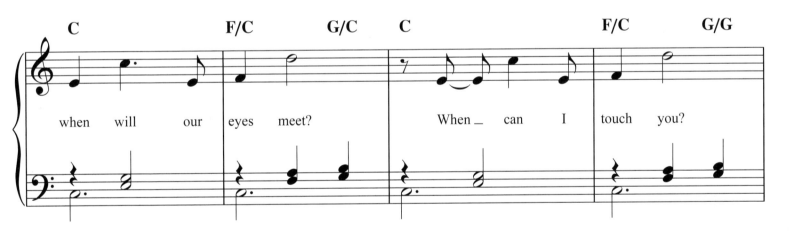

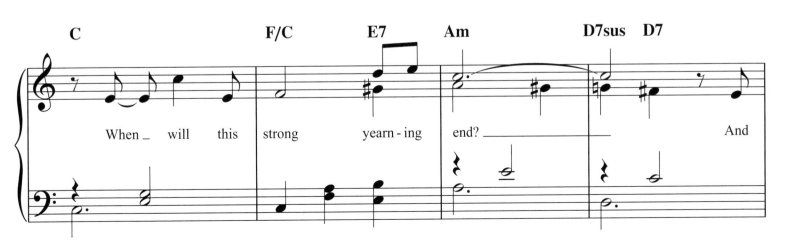

60

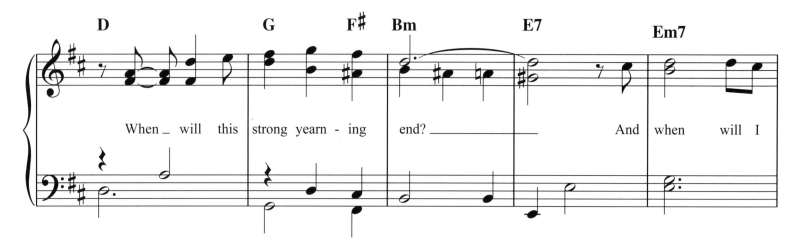

When __ will this strong yearn - ing end? _____

And when will I

hold you

rit.

mp a - gain?

a tempo

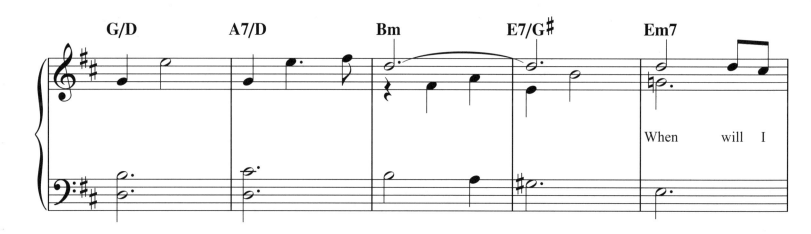

When will I

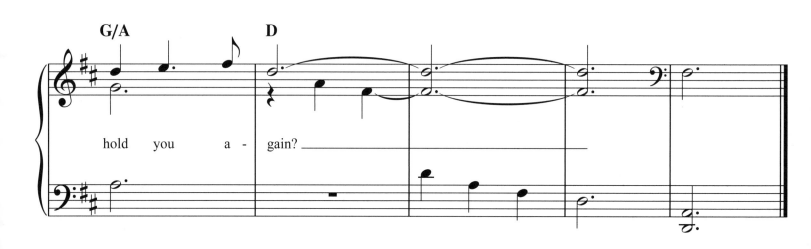

hold you a - gain? _____